Poems and Photographs

Kalina Fleming-López

2004

Copyright © 2014 Kalina Fleming-López

Pandora Lobo Estepario Productions

All rights reserved. No part of this book may be reproduced in any manner without the express written consent of the Publisher, except in the case of brief excerpts in critical reviews or articles. All inquiries should be addressed to: Pandora Lobo Estepario Productions, 1239 N. Greenview Ave. Chicago, IL 60642

All rights reserved.

ISBN-10: 1940856043
ISBN-13: 978-1-940856-04-9

Library of Congress Control Number:

DEDICATION

The publisher dedicates this book to all those who struggle to belong and are set aside by society and mores.

Contents

ACKNOWLEDGMENTS i
A church 7
Sideway pole 9
Little Swan 11
Annie 13
Perro 15
Me and Dad 17
This is Bilbao 19
You 21
The little City 23
DAD & MOM 25
ABOUT THE AUTHOR 27

ACKNOWLEDGMENTS

This book was written as a follow up to the young authors of the previous year. Kalina won that year's school competition and was trying to outdo herself with a self-designed, hand-bound book that included some of her photographs and poems. The judges did not believe that she had written the poems, taken the photographs and bound the book. We know she wrote the book, we were there. Kapra and Miguel.

Kalina Amelia Fleming-López

Photographs and Poems

A CHURCH

I see the church
the wind is blowing
people are walking
there are vines
I see the views of the church
the inside with all the glass
the church is so soft
the floor is so soft

it is made of moonstone
I am reading a book
while I am walking
through the hallway
and seems that never stops
I look back at me
I see two people
that look like my parents.

Kalina Amelia Fleming-López

SIDEWAY POLE

I see the pole
by the pole
I see the train leaving
I see my love leaving me
what can I do?
in the middle of the street
I see her leaving me
Into the distance

and the darkness
I see the church standing
and I saw the pole falling
there is a gate
that if anybody enters
they disappear
into the distance
that's where my love is gone.

Kalina Amelia Fleming-López

LITTLE SWAN

I saw the little swan
her eyes were made of gold
she flew into the distance
and she looked like the sun.

I saw the little swan
wings were made of silver
the water was not just like water

it was the cleanest, cleanest
water in the world.

I saw the little swan
Her legs were made of power
She swam like dust
Like herd of lions
That never stopped running
Like a cheetah, never stopping.

.

Kalina Amelia Fleming-López

ANNIE

I love my parents truly
You never'll get away with this
I look at you at my bed stand
And I look at your photo.
You know about my locket.
How can I stay in the orphanage?

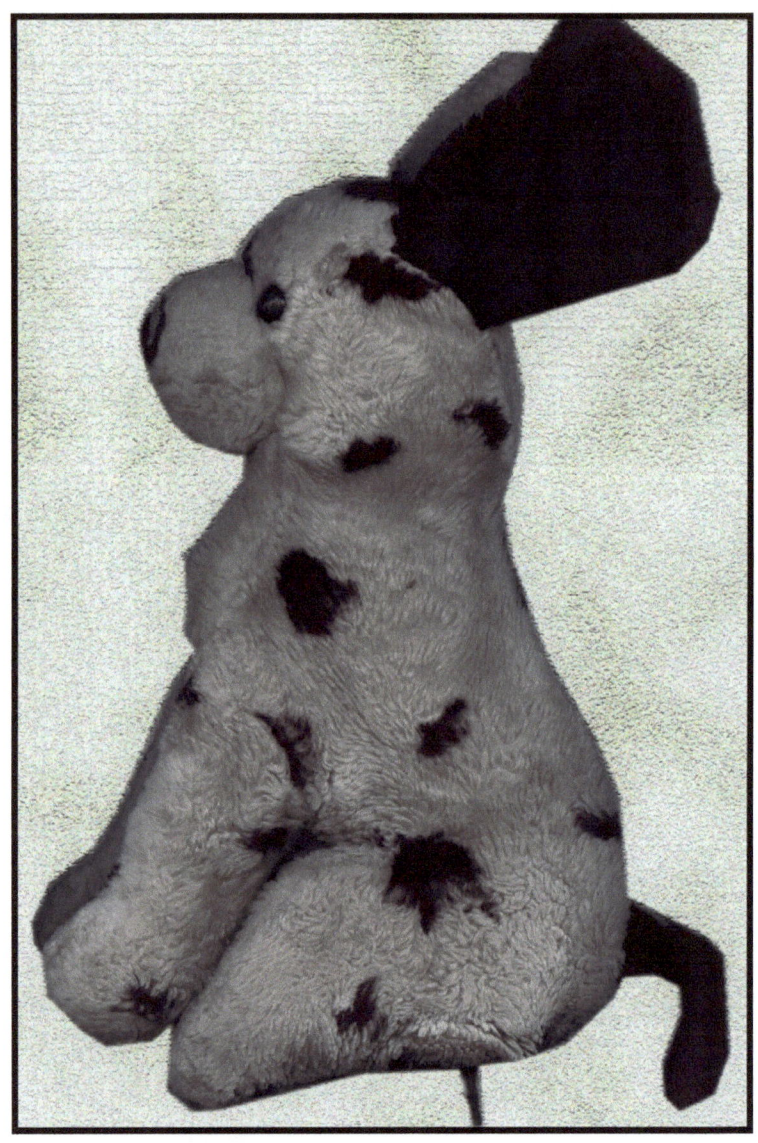

PERRO

Inside my soul
I see my Perro
Inside my hearth
I have Perro
Not one single night

I can stay without him
I look at the door
Perro is walking
beyond my dreams
he loves my family
because he is part of it.

ME AND DAD

Me and dad had great times
Together. When I was two
I couldn't talk but I just
Wanted to share with my
Dad. My dad and I were
Best friends. I loved
my father he is very nice
man he helps a lot.

Me and my Dad went to
Thousands of pyramids
when I was little. He's
a good cook. His name
is Miguel López-Lemus

THIS IS BILBAO

I see a train leaving
I love my parents truly
And look at the book of folders
I see my abuelito from México
Now I am looking at
The Webster's Universal Dictionary
It has six thousand words in it.
Now I am looking at the Michigan Lago
I see me wrapped-up in a towel
I say what I say
When I don't mean it
I can see me
Everywhere
I forgot what I said
in May
I see the skeletons coming
But they are leaving
There is no reason to be here
When I have my parents and cats.

YOU

I glimpse at myself
As I look at the stars
I see a little yellow kitten
he is on the top of the tower
 I glance at the stairway
and it goes round and round
Anyone that comes up
never comes down
if you have never seen the stairway
your skeleton gets smaller
your body gets bigger
until Midnight strikes.
The lion comes out
your bones are gone.
You are fatter than a balloon
you are fatter than an elephant
for tiger's dinner.
You do not have any other plans
In your life
you popped-up in the building
and broke it
But it always comes back
   Now that you are on a dungeon
you are squeezed
But you keep on getting fatter
and you never stop growing
Finally it stops
You are finally lions' dinner.

THE LITTLE CITY

I see the Padre of the Little City
There is a black cat
as he moves his arms
he takes away somebody's lunch from them
he finally downs the lunch
When he at last rests
is coming for winter's nap
As he glimpses around the city
 you can see he is on the top
of the Sears Tower
As he looks at a taxi cab
with a girl inside it
You do not know what he is thinking
He is thinking of an owner
where he gets a warm place to sleep
Maybe he'll find a family
He dreams and sleeps
that he got a full
breakfast, lunch and dinner
Hello Brother!!

Kalina Amelia Fleming-López

DAD & MOM

Maybe sometime I cast my afternoons
I cast the orchestra
I rule the wind
but I don't know why
It seems that is the only
little thing I have in my head
Why does everybody
have to have a talent?
It seems, not everybody has a talent
But my father and mother do.
Tonight is the night that I see Tonight
As I see the streets
I look at my mother and father
holding hands
walking down the street
I hear the ambulance calling
I do not know who it is
It is a mystery
I am walking around the poetry
Tonight I can look around the world
My parents
Are still not dead.

ABOUT THE AUTHOR

Kalina Amelia Fleming-López

Kalina Amelia Fleming-López is a third grade student at Inter-American Magnet School in Chicago.

"I write poems because I like it. I always wanted to be a poet for I have the talent from my father and mother."
January 11, 2004

www.ingramcontent.com/pod-product-compliance
Lightning Source LLC
Chambersburg PA
CBHW041809040426
42449CB00001B/29